39 Great Retirement Towns

From the Very Affordable to the Upscale

Written and Edited by Kris Kelley

Note:

Great effort has been made to verify the accuracy of the information in this book, but some information may have changed since publication. This especially applies to home prices and cost of living numbers in small towns as these are particularly sensitive to market changes. As a result, Webwerxx, Inc. cannot guarantee the accuracy of the content contained within this publication.

Cost of living numbers are primarily based on home prices but also include transportation costs, food costs, medical costs, utility costs and miscellaneous costs. For simplicity's sake, home prices and population numbers are rounded off.

It is also worth noting that some of these town may have been damaged by recent hurricanes. If so, then they will rebuild, as Florida towns always do.

Cover Image: © Artisticco LLC /123RF.COM

Table of Contents

Introduction

Florida is as popular as ever with retirees, thanks to its favorable tax structure, warm weather and beautiful beaches. Not all Florida towns, however, are created equal.

Here we have 39 Florida towns that are worth consideration when it comes to retirement. Some are well known. Others are off the radar. Twenty-two of them have a cost of living that meets the national average or is less than the national average. Seventeen of them have a cost of living that is higher than the national average.

Costs are primarily determined by housing prices. It is worth noting that real estate prices have greatly increased in the last year or two. Towns that have generally been considered inexpensive are still inexpensive compared to national averages, but they are pricier than they were a short time ago.

The towns with the lower costs are not fancy places, but they are safe and comfortable. The upscale towns have amenities and a quality of life that are worth the higher costs.

In each town, we look at population, median home price, percentage of people age 45 or better, medical facilities, transportation, climate, political leanings and more. And because no place is perfect, we also note each town's drawbacks.

It is also worth mentioning that Florida has less expensive towns than those in this book, but very inexpensive places tend to have high crime rates, poor infrastructure and/or population loss. We do not recommend these kinds of towns for retirement.

Towns with a Cost of Living Higher than the National Average

Apollo Beach

This unincorporated, canal-laced community is located on Florida's southwestern coast, about 20 miles south of Tampa. It is across the bay from St. Petersburg, south of Hillsborough Bay and has nearly doubled in size within the last 10 years.

Apollo Beach is primarily residential and has numerous named and gated subdivisions. Older neighborhoods mingle with new ones, and many homes, even ones reasonably priced, back to a canal and have a dock. Del Webb has a 55+ community here, too.

Parks in town include Covington Oak Park, Apollo Beach Park and the Wolf Branch Nature Preserve, which has acres of shoreline, coastal wetlands and picnic areas. The Sydney Dover Trails has a boat ramp and paths for hiking or horseback riding.

The town also rests in the shadow of the Big Bend Power Station, but residents have benefited from its proximity. TECO, the owners of the station, built a community events center that hosts the town's annual Manatee Festival of the Arts. The company also maintains a manatee viewing center.

The warm waters around the power station are a boon to winter fishing. Apollo Beach also has two marinas, both with wet and dry storage. The Tampa Sailing Squadron is headquartered in town and offers classes.

Residents enjoy some excellent restaurants. Many of these eateries are along the water.

Population: 25,000 (city proper)

Age 45 or Better: 48%

Cost of Living: 5% above the national average

Median Home Price: $450,000

Climate: Summer temperatures are in the 80s and 90s, and winter temperatures are in the 50s, 60s and 70s. The area, on average, receives 55 inches of rain per year.

At Least One Hospital Accepts Medicare Patients? No, but South Bay Hospital, four miles away in Sun City Center, accepts Medicare patients.

At Least One Hospital Accredited by Joint Commission?   No, but South Bay Hospital, four miles away in Sun City Center, is accredited.

Public Transit: Yes, provided by Gohart

Crime Rate: Below the national average

Public Library: No

Political Leanings: Liberal

Drawbacks: The tornado risk is 125% greater than the national average.

Notes: Apollo Beach is a quiet community and has 55 miles of canals.

Belle Isle

Leafy, down-to-earth and welcoming, Belle Isle is just six miles from downtown Orlando in east central Florida.   The town completely surrounds Lake Conway, which is one of several lakes in the Lake Conway Chain of Lakes. Two smaller lakes are within Belle Isle's borders as well.

With all this adjacent water, residents' weekends are busy with boating and fishing for bass, crappie, bream and more. The lakes are healthy, and the canals that connect them are well maintained. Residents enjoy four pretty parks, two of which have public beaches, and there is a boat launch area.

Older neighborhoods, many from the 1950s and 1960s, have flat roof, concrete block ranch ramblers, while newer areas have Mediterranean style and Craftsman style homes. Beautiful residences are located all along the lengthy shoreline.

Neighborhood-watch programs are active. The police department has a Senior Watch program that keeps an eye on the town's older residents, particularly when it comes to people who might want to scam them.

Shopping venues, restaurants and services are found next door in Orlando.

Population: 7,000 (city proper)

Age 45 or Better: 43%

Cost of Living: 19% above the national average

Median Home Price: $525,000

Climate: Summer temperatures are in the 80s and 90s, and winter temperatures are in the 40s, 50s and 60s. On average, the area receives 50 inches of rain per year.

At Least One Hospital Accepts Medicare Patients? No, but Orlando has several hospitals that accept Medicare patients.

At Least One Hospital Accredited by Joint Commission? No, but Orlando has several accredited hospitals.

Public Transit: Yes, although it is limited.

Crime Rate: Below the national average

Public Library: No

Political Leanings: Liberal

Drawbacks: None

Notes: Belle Isle is a nice town.

Boca Raton

Stylish Boca Raton sits along Florida's southeastern coast, about 20 miles north of Fort Lauderdale. A well-heeled metropolis, it is known for its upscale shopping venues and expensive, master-planned neighborhoods.

This is a well-maintained city with strict building codes that do not allow new billboards, car dealerships or flashy commercial advertising. Downtown's well known Mizner Park is a "lifestyle center" with an art museum, high end restaurants, elegant offices and exclusive, pastel-colored shops and boutiques.

Lush parks, manicured lawns, several golf courses, the Boca Ballet Theatre, the Boca Raton Philharmonic Symphony, a professional theater group and two miles of clean, white sand beaches are just a few of the amenities that contribute to Boca Raton's rich quality of life.

Three of the city's neighborhoods are among the most expensive gated communities in the nation. Homes with Mediterranean and Spanish Colonial architectural themes are particularly popular.

The city has a large, transplanted community of Northeasterners and is sometimes called the "sixth borough." This is a reference to the particularly high number of New Yorkers here.

Population: 98,000 (city proper)

Age 45 or Better: 45%

Cost of Living: 32% above the national average

Median Home Price: $625,000

Climate: This area has a tropical rainforest. Summer temperatures are in the 80s and 90s, and winter temperatures are in the 50s and 60s. On average, the area receives 60 inches of rain per year.

At Least One Hospital Accepts Medicare Patients? Yes

At Least One Hospital Accredited by Joint Commission? Yes

Public Transit: Yes, provided by Palm Tran

Crime Rate: Meets the national average

Public Library: Yes

Political Leanings: Liberal

Drawbacks: Hurricanes and tropical storms can happen.

Notes: Boca Raton has a reputation for bad drivers and was once a favorite organized crime hangout. Winter tourists come in droves.

Coral Springs

Bordered by the Everglades, sprawling Coral Springs sits in southeastern Florida, about 20 miles northwest of Fort Lauderdale

and about 11 miles inland from the Atlantic Ocean. It started out as a master-planned development in the 1960s and grew rapidly in the 1970s, 1980s and 1990s.

The growth slowed considerably during the last decade or so, but the city still wins praise for its quality of life and family friendliness. Generally, residents are educated and affluent, and the city is well maintained and well governed.

Coral Springs is also known for its architectural aesthetics and strict building codes and landscaping codes. These regulate everything from exterior paint colors and commercial signs to boat storage and roofing materials. McDonald's was not even allowed to have its iconic golden arches signage.

The city has a good parks system and a good school system. The downtown is in the middle of an extensive redevelopment project. Restaurants of all types are in abundance, and the Mega Green Market is a year-round farmers' market.

Residents enjoy two shopping malls and a community theater. The Coral Springs Center for the Arts hosts touring Broadway shows. The biggest event of the year is the Coral Springs Festival of the Arts in March.

Housing is a good mix of single-family homes, town homes and condominiums.

Population: 135,000 (city proper)

Age 45 or Better: 35%

Cost of Living: 26% above the national average

Median Home Price: $565,000

Climate: Summers are hot and humid with temperatures in the 80s and 90s, and winters are mild with temperatures in the 50s, 60s and 70s. On average, the area receives 68 inches of rain each year.

At Least One Hospital Accepts Medicare Patients? Yes

At Least One Accredited by Joint Commission?   Yes

Public Transit: Yes

Crime Rate: Below the national average

Public Library: Yes. It is part of the Broward County system.

Political Leanings: Liberal

Drawbacks: This area is prone to hurricanes, and Coral Springs can feel storm effects even though it is inland.

Notes: Coral Springs is a nice city and has landed on "best places to live" lists.

Doctor Phillips

Located 10 miles southwest of Orlando in central Florida, pleasant Doctor Phillips was named after an early, innovative citrus titan, Dr. Phillip Phillips.   It is an unincorporated town with a good reputation.

Three lakes in the Butler Chain of Lakes are within town limits, and boating and water sports are a way of life for many residents. Neighborhoods, many gated, are lush and well-manicured, and orange trees once planted by "Doc" Phillips still line some streets.

Single family housing stock is comprised mostly of Mediterranean styles and concrete block ranch ramblers. Condominiums are in good supply, too.

The city has worked to control growth and maintain its infrastructure, and residents are happy with Doctor Phillips' quality of life. The school system has an excellent reputation, and the high school football team is a particular point of pride.

The Marketplace at Dr. Phillips is located on Sand Lake Road, a major east-west thoroughfare. This is also the site of Restaurant Row, where nearly any type of nicer eatery can be found.

Population: 12,000 (city proper)

Age 45 or Better: 30%

Cost of Living: 27% above the national average

Median Home Price: $575,000

Climate: Summer temperatures are in the 80s and 90s with frequent rainstorms. Winter temperatures are in the 60s and 70s. On average, the area receives 51 inches of rain per year.

At Least One Hospital Accepts Medicare Patients? Yes

At Least One Hospital Accredited by Joint Commission? Yes

Public Transit: Yes, but it is limited.

Crime Rate: Below the national average

Public Library: Yes

Political Leanings: Liberal

Drawbacks: None

Notes: Disney World is just five miles to the southwest.

Estero

Once inhabited by Native American Calusas and treasure seeking Spaniards, Estero was founded as a religious colony and Utopian society in the late 19th century. It sits along Estero Bay in southwestern Florida and has been growing very quickly.

Although Estero did not flourish as a Utopian community, its pretty beaches, abundant wildlife and vast opportunities for recreation still make it a desirable place to live. Established neighborhoods with ranch ramblers now coexist with sleek new subdivisions peppered with Mediterranean style homes and Italian influenced architecture.

Residents enjoy kayaking, canoeing, boating, fishing and other water activities. Weekend festivals and events include the CREW Wildflower Show, golf expositions and the Mound Key Paddle Tour.

Several museums and galleries are devoted to the local Native American and Utopian history. Mound Key Archeological State Park, a rich Calusa artifact site, is only accessible by boat. Koreshan State Historic Site is the location of the original religious settlement.

Two large malls provide excellent shopping opportunities. A new, upscale mixed-use development is planned for the downtown area.

Population: 38,000 (city proper)

Age 45 or Better: 70%

Cost of Living: 26% above the national average

Median Home Price: $570,000

Climate: Summer temperatures are in the 80s and 90s, and winter temperatures are in the 50s, 60s and 70s. On average, the area receives 48 inches of rain per year.

At Least One Hospital Accepts Medicare Patients? No, but Gulf Coast Medical Center is eight miles away in Fort Myers and accepts Medicare patients.

At Least One Hospital Accredited by Joint Commission? No, but Gulf Coast Medical Center is eight miles away in Fort Myers and is accredited.

Public Transit: Yes, provided by LeeTran, but it is limited.

Crime Rate: Below the national average

Public Library: Yes

Political Leanings: Conservative

Drawbacks: Hurricanes are always a possibility.

Notes: None

Geneva

Peaceful Geneva, an unincorporated town in northeastern Florida, is proud of its history and its rural roots.   Although it is only 20 miles from Orlando, it is surrounded by water and wilderness and feels a world away.   In fact, locals sometimes refer to it as "the lost world." Both the big and little Econlockhatchee River flow nearby.

Many residences sit on large, somewhat overgrown, country lots, and long dirt driveways are common.   Home styles range from plantation and ranch rambler to Spanish Colonial.

The several lakes within town are mostly in their natural state with little development around them.   The Little Big Econ State Forest's 9,600 acres have a 12-mile single track bike trail, canoe put-ins and multiple areas for hiking, bird watching and horseback riding.

Geneva also abuts the Lake Harney Wilderness Area, which has 300 acres of Native American shell middens, floodplain marshes and bald eagle nests.

The historical society runs a museum with artifacts from the Ice Age to the ferry and railroad age.   The Rural Heritage Center, housed in the town's brick schoolhouse, offers gun safety tips, basket making workshops and theater classes.

The town has a couple of general stores, a feed store and a meat market. Most shopping is done in nearby Oviedo or Sanford.

Population: 3,300 (city proper)

Age 45 or Better: 34%

Cost of Living: 25% above the national average

Median Home Price: $565,000

Climate: Summer temperatures are in the 80s and 90s. Winter temperatures are in the 50s, 60s and 70s. Average rainfall is 52 inches per year with the usual summertime afternoon showers.

At Least One Hospital Accepts Medicare Patients? No, but Central Florida Regional Hospital, 10 miles away in Sanford, accepts Medicare patients.

At Least One Accredited by Joint Commission? No, but Central Florida Regional Hospital, 10 miles away in Sanford, is accredited. It is also a teaching hospital.

Public Transit: No

Crime Rate: Below the national average

Public Library: No

Political Leanings: Nearly split down the middle

Drawbacks: The tornado risk is 90% above the national average.

Notes: Geneva is very low key and is the kind of place where residents turn out with lawn chairs for a bridge dedication.

Hernando Beach

Hernando Beach was developed in the 1960s and sits along Florida's west coast, about an hour north of Tampa. Dredged from wetlands and the Gulf of Mexico's floor, it is a remote place laced with canals.

This is primarily a residential community, and despite its name, it does not have a beach. Instead, it has great inshore fishing, offshore fishing and a yacht club.

The north end of the town has direct Gulf access, and the Hernando Beach Marina hosts shrimp boats and pleasure craft. It also has fishing charters, high and dry storage, repair facilities and dockside eateries.

Homes are a mix of beautiful Mediterranean styles and modest ranch ramblers. Nearly all residences back to a canal.

The Weekiwachee Preserve sits on the eastern edge of town and has a patchwork of habitats, including pine covered sandhills, hardwood hammocks, river frontage and marshes. It is home to a large population of black bears and numerous bird species. Hiking paths, biking trails and fishing lakes are scattered throughout the Preserve.

Nearby Spring Hill has a variety of national retailers and local shops.

Population: 2,600 (city proper)

Age 45 or Better: 64%

Cost of Living: 34% above the national average

Median Home Price: $610,000

Climate: Summer temperatures are in the 80s and 90s. Winter temperatures are in the 60s and 70s. On average, the area receives 50 inches of rain per year.

At Least One Hospital Accepts Medicare Patients? No, but Regional Medical Center Bayonet Point, about eight miles away in Hudson, accepts Medicare patients.

At Least One Hospital Accredited by Joint Commission? No, but Regional Medical Center Bayonet Point, about eight miles away in Hudson, is accredited.

Public Transit: No

Crime Rate: Well below the national average

Public Library: No, but Spring Hill, about 10 miles away, has a library.

Political Leanings: Conservative

Drawbacks: The tornado risk is 80% higher than the national average.

Notes: None

Highland Beach

Highland Beach, a balmy beach community along State Road A1A in southeastern Florida, is framed by the Intracoastal Waterway and the Atlantic Ocean.   It was settled by Japanese immigrants in the early 20th century and incorporated in 1949.

With only 1.1 square miles of land to its name, Highland Beach is walkable from end to end, and it does not have a single traffic light. The library is a cultural hub and offers art exhibitions, concerts, book groups, mahjong and movies.

Delray Beach and Boca Raton rest on the town's southern and northern borders. Amenities in these larger communities include restaurants, shopping venues, the Gumbo Limbo Nature Center and the Delray Beach Center for the Arts.

The Everglades and the Loxahatchee National Wildlife Reserve are within easy reach and permit boating, hiking and fishing. The nearby Yamato Scrub Natural Area has trails that wander through five ecosystems. Spanish River Park allows camping, picnicking and swimming.

Tall, white condominiums and gorgeous single-family homes overlook both the Atlantic Ocean and the Intracoastal Waterway. Sea turtles also make their nests on the Atlantic shore.

Population: 4,500 (city proper)

Age 45 or Better: 81%

Cost of Living: 78% above the national average

Median Home Price: $850,000

Climate: This area has a tropical monsoon climate. The area receives 58 inches of rain per year, on average.

At Least One Hospital Accepts Medicare Patients? No, but Boca Raton Regional Hospital is within five miles and accepts Medicare patients.

At Least One Hospital is Accredited by Joint Commission? No, but Boca Raton Regional Hospital is within five miles and is accredited.

Public Transit: No, although the County has a program to transport the disabled to a shelter in the event of a hurricane.

Crime Rate: Well below the national average

Public Library: Yes

Political Leanings: Very liberal

Drawbacks: Hurricanes are always a possibility.

Hobe Sound

In 1696, a ship carrying British Quakers sank off Florida's southeastern coast, and the religious group was forced ashore. It was the first time that white men had set eyes upon the idyllic area now known as Hobe Sound.

Residents have eight golf courses from which to choose, and restaurants include catfish houses, BBQ places, steakhouses and delis. A Publix and a Winn Dixie are also here.

Housing is an interesting mix. Established, organic neighborhoods have small, older homes on leafy streets. Other areas have newly planted trees and expensive, celebrity owned waterfront estates.

Hobe Sound's best feature may be its secret beach, a long stretch of pristine, nearly empty sand within the nearby Hobe Sound National Wildlife Refuge. There is no development around, and the only amenities are an observation platform and a parking area. The views of unspoiled sand, surf and sky are breathtaking.

Other nature areas are close at hand, too. Rambling Jonathan Dickinson State Park has camping areas. Saint Lucie Inlet Preserve State Park has a scenic kayak trail. Blowing Rocks Preserve is a popular snorkeling destination.

Population: 15,000 (city proper)

Age 45 or Better: 58%

Cost of Living: 21% above the national average

Median Home Price: $540,000

Climate: This area sits in a transition zone between tropical and subtropical climates. On average, the area receives 57 inches of rain per year.

At Least One Hospital Accepts Medicare Patients? No, but Martin Memorial is seven miles away in Stuart and accepts Medicare patients.

At Least One Hospital Accredited by Joint Commission? No, but Martin Memorial seven miles away in Stuart and is accredited.

Public Transit: There is a dial-a-ride van service but no fixed public bus route.

Crime Rate: Below the national average

Public Library: Yes

Political Leanings: Conservative

Drawbacks: Hurricanes are always a possibility.

Notes: Hobe Sound is sometimes considered an exurb of Port St. Lucie to the north.

Lauderdale-by-the-Sea

Laid back Lauderdale-by-the-Sea, located on a barrier island just east of Fort Lauderdale on Florida's southeastern coast, is home to sunny beaches and coral reefs. It dates from the 1920s.

The community has worked to limit high rise hotels and condominium developments and maintains a bohemian but prosperous vibe. Palm trees line the streets, and single story, white and pastel-colored buildings glisten in the sun.

Vacationers come in droves to snorkel, swim, Jet Ski, soak up rays and SCUBA dive. A favorite dive spot is the SS Copenhagen, a 19th century cargo steamer in twenty-five feet of water just 100 yards offshore.

The beaches are clean, often crowded and home to loggerhead sea turtle nesting grounds. The long wooden pier is usually occupied by fishermen, and open air, thatch roof beach bars do a steady business.

Taste of the Beach, movie nights and Swing by the Sea are just a few of the town's fun events. Residents also take part in dune restoration projects and beach clean-up days.

Neighborhoods are neatly laid out, and homes, many of which back to a canal, are a mix of Florida cracker style, concrete block style and Mediterranean style. Apartments and condominiums are in good supply, too.

Busy North Ocean Drive (Highway A1A) and Commercial Boulevard are lined with banks, stores, gas stations, shopping centers and much more.

Population: 6,300 (city proper)

Age 45 or Better: 55%

Cost of Living: 45% above the national average

Median Home Price: $675,000

Climate: Summer temperatures reach into the 90s, and winters stay mild with temperatures in the 50s, 60s and 70s. On average, the area receives 60 inches of rain per year.

At Least One Hospital Accepts Medicare Patients? No, but Imperial Medical Center is one mile away and accepts Medicare patients.

At Least One Hospital Accredited by Joint Commission? No, but Imperial Medical Center is one mile away and is accredited.

Public Transit: Yes, the Pelican Hopper, a free bus/van, makes a 45-minute loop around town and stops at a grocery, the hospital and more.

Crime Rate: Below the national average

Public Library: No

Political Leanings: Very liberal

Drawbacks: None

Notes: Spring Breakers come to party in March and April.

Marco Island

Just off the southwestern Florida coast, upscale Marco Island is a town on a barrier island of the same name. It is located at the northern end of a string of islands called Ten Thousand Islands and is connected to the mainland via the Jolley Bridge. Resort development began in the 1960s, and today Marco Island has a contemporary, tropical vibe.

The city is somewhat isolated and is one of the last communities on the southwestern coast before the land is overtaken by subtropical wetlands (the Everglades). Even so, Marco Island's population doubles in size during the winter. Six miles of sparkling white beaches and bright blue waters that are some of the most stunning along the Florida coast are the reasons why.

Tall condominiums line the beach, and wild bobcats have even been spotted lounging on the sand.   The city's central area is surrounded by neighborhoods laced with 100 miles of canals and waterways. Many homes, modern and elegant, sit along the water and have a boat dock.

Residents enjoy a boat parade each December and a farmers' market from November through April. Eateries range from sandwich shops to sophisticated, fine dining establishments.

Population: 19,000 (city proper)

Age 45 or Better: 65%

Cost of Living: 105% above the national average

Median Home Price: $998,000

Climate: Marco Island has a tropical wet and dry climate, with most rain coming between June and October. Summer temperatures are in the 80s and 90s, and winter temperatures are in the 60s and 70s.

At Least One Hospital Accepts Medicare Patients? No, but Physicians Regional in Naples is 10 to 15 miles away, depending on the campus, and accepts Medicare patients.

At Least One Hospital Accredited by Joint Commission? No, but Physicians Regional in Naples is 10 to 15 miles away, depending on the campus, and is accredited.

Public Transit: Yes, provided by Collier Area Transit. A high-speed ferry travels to Key West.

Crime Rate: Well below the national average

Public Library: Yes

Political Leanings: Very conservative

Drawbacks: This area is susceptible to hurricanes and storm surges, and Marco Island is completely exposed.

Notes: The area has two beaches. One has facilities and the other does not. Marco Island is home to a handful of celebrities and professional athletes.

Melbourne Beach

One of Brevard County's oldest seaside communities, the mostly residential town of Melbourne Beach sits on a barrier island. Unhurried and quaint, it is known for its beautiful stretches of beaches.

Inland homes sit along palm lined streets neatly laid out along grids. On the Atlantic side, tall, white-washed condominium buildings with beachfront pools edge the sand, while the river side is dotted with large Mediterranean style residences with long piers and boat docks. Aquarina Country Club is the island's only gated golf development.

Businesses include bait shops, colorful terraced seafood restaurants and a couple of local markets. The heart of Melbourne Beach is Ryckman Park, home to the town hall, the community center and the Melbourne Beach Pier.

The Juan Ponce de Leon Landing, built to commemorate the explorer's American arrival, is a pretty beach park with mangrove-packed dunes and walkways. The Barrier Island Center has an observation deck, interactive exhibits and ongoing education programs.

Locals and tourists alike come out for the annual Melbourne Main Street Fall Festival. This signature event features arts, crafts, food, music and draws up to 50,000 visitors

The area has two golf courses, the Spessard Holland course and the Aquarina Country Club course. The nearby Archie Carr National Wildlife is a refuge for Loggerhead turtles and has foot trails, a kayak launch and tours.

Population: 3,500 (city proper)

Age 45 or Better: 51%

Cost of Living: 59% above the national average

Median Home Price: $750,000

Climate: This area has a humid subtropical climate. On average, Melbourne Beach receives 55 inches of rain per year.

At Least One Hospital Accepts Medicare Patients? No, but Melbourne, three miles away, has a hospital that accepts Medicare patients.

At Least One Hospital Accredited by Joint Commission? No, but Melbourne, three miles away, has a hospital that is accredited and a primary stroke center.

Public Transit: No, but a private shuttle has service to neighboring towns.

Crime Rate: Well below the national average

Public Library: Yes

Political Leanings: Conservative

Drawbacks: The area is completely exposed if a hurricane or tropical storm should hit.

Notes: The Melbourne Causeway is the road to the mainland, and it can become clogged with traffic during the summer.

Miramar Beach

Mesmerizing turquoise waters and miles of sugar white sand are what lure people to sun drenched Miramar Beach. It is a classic seaside community nestled along Florida's Panhandle.

The beach is lined with tall, white-washed hotels and condominiums. The water views are breathtaking.

Neighborhoods, many without sidewalks, are lush and neatly planned. Housing consists of pastel-colored bungalows, short and tall condominiums, Mediterranean style estates, three story homes with triple balconies and more.

Beach eateries include crab shacks, oyster bars, pizza joints, sandwich shops and Thai places.

Shopping venues are primarily antique stores, beach accessory shops and a Winn Dixie. Silver Sands Factory Stores, one of the nation's largest outlet malls, is next door in Destin.

Population: 9,000 (city proper)

Age 45 or Better: 60%

Cost of Living: 44% above the national average

Median Home Price: $665,000

Climate: The area has a humid subtropical climate. Summer temperatures are in the 80s and 90s, and winter temperatures are in the 50s, 60s and 70s. On average, Miramar Beach receives 65 inches of rain per year.

At Least One Hospital Accepts Medicare Patients? Yes

At Least One Hospital Accredited by Joint Commission? Yes

Public Transit: No

Crime Rate: Below the national average

Public Library: No, but Destin has a library.

Political Leanings: Very conservative

Drawbacks: If a hurricane hits, the town has no protection.

Notes: The town is a census designated place, not an incorporated town, and is often mistakenly considered an extension of neighboring Destin nine miles to the west.   Miramar Beach also has an RV park.

Naples

With palm trees swaying, pastel -buildings glistening and sea air wafting, beautiful Naples is a wealthy, sun drenched coastal town with a "beachy" resort ambiance.   It is on Florida's southwestern coast and is a noted vacation destination, attracting a stylish, well-heeled tourist crowd. Shopping, dining, plenty of golf and all kinds of water recreation are why people come here.

Neighborhoods tend to cater to one of two demographics, part time owners or year-round owners.   Part time owner neighborhoods are often gated, expensive and dotted with amenities that may include a golf course, tennis courts and more.   Neighborhoods that are popular with year-round locals lack amenities but are more affordable.

Downtown Naples has brick streets lined by high end boutiques and other retailers. 5th Avenue South and 3rd Street South are particularly fashionable.

Gallery Row appeals to upscale antique hunters, while several open-air shopping districts along Naples Bay are perfect for fine dining, shopping, and strolling and people watching.

Naples calls itself the "Golf Capital of the World," and it claims to have more golf holes per capita than anywhere else in the country. Ninety-five courses within 30 miles of downtown, and many courses are located within country clubs.

The 10-mile-long beach is clean, sugar white and usually crowded. It has been voted one of America's best beaches and is lined by tall condominiums.

One spot, pretty Delnor-Wiggins Pass State Recreation Area, is located on a barrier island and is free of commercial development. It is one of the most popular parks in southwestern Florida.

The Philharmonic Center for the Arts presents a Best of Broadway series, dance recitals, classical music and much more. Theater buffs are well served by TheatreZone, a professional equity group, and by the Naples Players, a community theater group.

A zoo, a library, a botanic garden, Christmas boat parades and beachside concerts further ensure that there is always something to do.

Population: 21,000 (city proper)

Age 45 or Better: 72%

Cost of Living: 47% above the national average

Median Home Price: $685,000

Climate: Summer temperatures are in the 80s and 90s with high humidity levels and frequent rainstorms. Winter temperatures are in the 60s and 70s. On average, the area receives 55 inches of rain per year.

At Least One Hospital Accepts Medicare Patients? Yes

At Least One Hospital Accredited by Joint Commission? Yes

Public Transit: Yes

Crime Rate: Well below the national average

Public Library: Yes

Political Leanings: Very conservative

Drawbacks: None

Notes: Naples has a reputation as being somewhat snobby, and tourist traffic is heavy from November through April.

Nokomis

The unincorporated beach town of Nokomis is situated between Sarasota and Venice on Florida's southwestern coast.   It reminds many people of what Florida used to be and has a relaxed Gulf Coast ambiance.

Some parts of town are wooded, undeveloped and a little bedraggled with dilapidated rentals and beach shacks. Other areas have expensive single-family homes. Palm trees, oak trees and pine trees shade most neighborhoods.

There are several gated communities, and those on Casey Key may be the most well-known. This eight-mile-long barrier island has some of the most expensive real estate in Florida. It is peppered with large, multi-million-dollar beachfront estates, and celebrities of various sorts make their home here.

Tourists seem to bypass Nokomis and head instead to nearby Sarasota, so local restaurants and roads are not terribly crowded in the winter. Residents enjoy seafood diners, cafes and at least one Italian bistro.

Nokomis Beach, pristine, long and white, is caressed by water a seductive shade of green. Boaters, Jet Skiers, swimmers and water skiers are active year-round. The beach has a boardwalk and free parking.

Thirty-three golf courses are within a short drive, and downtown Sarasota is 15 miles away.

Population: 4,200 (city proper)

Age 45 or Better: 53%

Cost of Living: 34% above the national average

Median Home Price: $610,000

Climate: Summer temperatures are in the 80s and 90s with high humidity levels and frequent rainstorms. Winter temperatures are in the 60s and 70s.

At Least One Hospital Accepts Medicare Patients? No, but Venice Regional Medical Center is about five miles away and accepts Medicare patients.

At Least One Hospital Accredited by Joint Commission? No, but Venice Regional Medical Center is about five miles away and is accredited.

Public Transit: There is no public transportation within town, but SCAT has a bus that runs north to Sarasota and south to Venice.

Crime Rate: Below the national average

Public Library: No

Political Leanings: Conservative

Drawbacks: None

Notes: Services not found in town can be found about five miles away in Venice.

Windermere

Secluded, upscale Windermere is just outside of Orlando in east central Florida. It is located on an isthmus in the Butler Chain of Lakes, eleven bodies of water recognized for their high-water quality and wildlife.

The town is known for its tree canopied dirt roads, understated atmosphere and elegant waterfront residences. A few celebrities and Orlando Magic basketball players make Windermere their home.

Residents are protective of their country hamlet and work to keep much of the outside world at bay. The town regulates the traffic that travels through it from one side of the lake Chain to the other and encourages drivers to use alternate routes.

The downtown is cozy and quaint. Locals ensure that it stays that way through strict building and zoning codes.

Annual festivals include the Windermere Craft Beer Fest and the Festival Among the Lakes, which consists of a wakeboarding competition and boat show. Proceeds from the Lakes event go to charity.

When it comes to dining out, critically acclaimed bistros mingle with fast food chains. Residents travel to Orlando for most shopping and services.

Population: 3,000 (city proper)

Age 45 or Better: 41%

Cost of Living: 53% above the national average

Median Home Price: $725,000

Climate: Summers and early fall are warm and rainy with temperatures in the 80s and 90s.   Late fall and winter are generally dry and sunny with temperatures in the 50s, 60s and 70s.

At Least One Hospital Accepts Medicare Patients? No, but Orlando has several hospitals that accept Medicare patients.

At Least One Hospital Accredited by Joint Commission?   No, but Orlando has several hospitals that are accredited.

Public Transit: No

Crime Rate: Well below the national average

Public Library: Yes, and it is in a Florida cracker style building with a wraparound porch.

Political Leanings: Liberal

Drawbacks: The tornado risk is 135% higher than the national average.

Notes: The Magic Kingdom's nightly fireworks can be seen from many a Windermere front porch.

Towns with a Cost of Living Less than or Equal to the National Average

Bayonet Point

Quiet Bayonet Point is on Florida's rural west central coast, about 45 minutes north of Tampa. Unincorporated and residential, no one seems to know how it got its name.

Werner-Boyce Salt Springs State Park, a 320-foot-deep salt marsh, sits directly to the west of Bayonet Point and creates a buffer

between the town and the Gulf of Mexico. Teeming with wildlife, the Park has hiking trails and fishing spots but no beaches or swimming areas.

Some homes back directly to the Park, but most residences are in modest, named neighborhoods that are neatly laid out on a grid. Dwellings are primarily wood frame structures or concrete block ranch ramblers, and many neighborhoods are deed restricted with a homeowners' association.

A golf club and at least one shopping center are here, but most services, restaurants and shopping areas are in Hudson, about four miles to the north.

Population: 28,000 (city proper)

Age 45 or Better: 62%

Cost of Living: 31% below the national average

Median Home Price: $255,000

Climate: Summer temperatures are in the 80s and 90s, and winter temperatures are in the 60s and 70s. On average, the area receives 52 inches of rain per year.

At Least One Hospital Accepts Medicare Patients? No, but Regional Medical Center is three miles away in Hudson and accepts Medicare patients.

At Least One Hospital Accredited by Joint Commission? No, but Regional Medical Center is three miles away in Hudson and is accredited.

Public Transit: No

Crime Rate: Meets the national average

Public Library: No

Political Leanings: Conservative

Drawbacks: Hurricanes are always a possibility.

Notes: None

Beverly Beach

This tiny, tightly knit Flagler County town is only 1.3 miles long and sits on a barrier island between the Matanzas River and the Atlantic Ocean on Florida's northeastern coast. Scenic Highway A1A runs through it.

Primarily residential with a beautiful beach, Beverly Beach has older seaside homes, some condominiums and Surfside Estates, a large, compact mobile home park for people age 55 or better. Sunset Inlet is a new housing development with conch style homes and boat docks.

Camptown RV Resort sits between A1A and the ocean. It has a general store, but most shopping and commercial services are in Flagler Beach or Palm Coast, the town's next-door neighbors.

Herschel King Park has a riverside boat ramp and canoe launch. Fishing is permitted on the beach and on the riverside seawall.

Nearby attractions include the Graham Swamp Conservation Area and the Washington Oaks State Park. The centerpiece of Washington Oaks is a formal garden, but there are also short trails for hiking and biking.

Population: 500 (city proper)

Age 45 or Better: 80%

Cost of Living: 12% below the national average

Median Home Price: $350,000

Climate: Summer temperatures are in the 80s and 90s, and winter temperatures are in the 50s, 60s and 70s. On average, Beverly Beach receives 50 inches of rain per year.

At Least One Hospital Accepts Medicare Patients? No, but Florida Hospital Flagler, four miles away in Palm Coast, accepts Medicare patients.

At Least One Hospital Accredited by Joint Commission? No, but Florida Hospital Flagler, four miles away in Palm Coast, is accredited.

Public Transit: Flagler County Public Transportation has an on-demand van system that runs through the County.

Crime Rate: Well below the national average

Public Library: No

Political Leanings: Conservative

Drawbacks: The town is completely exposed if a hurricane should strike.

Notes: The RV resort is popular with "snowbirds." Even though Beverly Beach is tiny, it has a mayor, commissioners and a town hall. Flagler Beach's senior center, which is just down the road, provides hot lunches, computer help and has a lending library.

Briny Breezes

Located directly east of Boynton Beach on Florida's southeastern coast, Briny Breezes is a mobile home park that is an incorporated town. It is wedged between the Intracoastal Waterway and the Atlantic Ocean and has a very mature demographic.

This tiny place got its start as a strawberry field in the 1920s. The owner of the field began leasing lots to northerners who came south to camp for the winter, and in the 1950s, he sold the lots to the campers. In 1963, they in turn incorporated the trailer park into a town with a post office and a mayor.

Briny Breezes has not changed much since then. All residences are white colored mobile homes, and they are neatly laid out and tightly packed together. Some of them back to one of four canals and have a boat dock.

The town has a clubhouse, a private beach and a good menu of clubs and planned activities. The Curtain Raisers produce a theatrical event each season. The Beach Club hosts Wednesday evening happy hours and has a long, oceanfront deck. The Art League offers painting classes, and the Travel Club lets residents give presentations about their recent travel adventures.

Restaurants, shops, groceries, banks, gas stations, churches and the like are found next door in Boynton Beach.

Population: 550 (city proper)

Age 45 or Better: 90%

Cost of Living: 8% below the national average

Median Home Price: $375,000

Climate: Summer temperatures are in the 80s and 90s, and winter temperatures are in the 60s and 70s. On average, the area receives 58 inches of rain per year.

At Least One Hospital Accepts Medicare Patients? No, but Bethesda Memorial in Boynton Beach accepts Medicare patients.

At Least One Accredited by Joint Commission? No, but Bethesda Memorial in Boynton Beach is accredited.

Public Transit: No

Crime Rate: Below the national average

Public Library: No

Political Leanings: Liberal

Drawbacks: Briny Breezes is completely exposed if a hurricane should strike.

Notes: Many residents are "snowbirds," down from the Northeast and Canada for the winter. Briny Breezes has 488 homes, few of which are new. Every homeowner owns shares in the town.

Carrabelle

Carrabelle is a working fishing village and deep-water seaport on the eastern Florida Panhandle. It dates from 1877 and sits at the convergence of three rivers and the Gulf of Mexico. Surrounded by water, open land and forests, Carrabelle exudes an old-fashioned Florida vibe.

Harvesting seafood remains a way of life for many residents, with shrimpers and oystermen heading out to sea each morning. Sport fishing tourism helps support the local economy, with grouper, snapfish and tarpon in good supply. The waterfront is lengthy and authentic.

Although the downtown is a little nondescript, it has a grocery and deli, a seafood market, a hardware store, a gift shop and the "World's Smallest Police Station," which is a 1963 phone booth that is now a tourist attraction. The annual Riverfront Festival brings nearly everyone out for food and people watching.

The beach, Carrabelle Beach, is just to the west and is clean, quiet and unspoiled by development. Dog Island's strips of sand, which are just offshore, are particularly enticing.

Tate's Hell State Forest and Apalachicola State Forest border Carrabelle to the north and are the place for camping, hiking and biking. They are also teeming with wildlife.

Neighborhoods are rural, and homes range from shacks and cottages to nice, brick ranch ramblers.

Population: 3,000 (city proper)

Age 45 or Better: 44%

Cost of Living: 26% below the national average

Median Home Price: $275,000

Climate: Summer temperatures are in the 80s and 90s. Winters have temperatures in the 60s and 70s. On average, the area receives 56 inches of rain per year.

At Least One Hospital Accepts Medicare Patients? Yes

At Least One Hospital Accredited by Joint Commission? No. The nearest accredited hospital is in Tallahassee, 50 miles away.

Public Transit: No

Crime Rate: Below the national average

Public Library: Yes

Political Leanings: Very conservative

Drawbacks: The area has been struck by at least three hurricanes, the latest being Michael in 2018, which caused significant damage.

Notes: Many residents travel to Tallahassee 50 miles away along country roads, for shopping and services. Weems Memorial Hospital is not accredited but has a heliport for fast transport to Tallahassee if needed.

Citrus Springs

This unincorporated town lies near the northern edge of Citrus County in northwestern Florida and began in the 1970s as a Mackle family real estate venture. Today it is a modest, remote subdivision with a mature demographic.

Many home sites are still for sale, so the community has a wooded, natural feeling about it. Some neighborhoods are developed and densely populated while others are not. Residences are primarily ranch ramblers with stucco exteriors. Wildlife is abundant and for the most part coexists peacefully with humans.

Residents enjoy a variety of activities, including a Red Hat Society chapter and a calligraphy guild. These are sponsored by the Citrus Springs Community Center and Civic Association. There are thirty parks, and golfers have 36 holes to enjoy at two country clubs.

The community is one of the trailheads for the Withlacoochee State Trail, a 46-mile-long path that meanders through small towns, ranches and natural areas. Nearby Springs State Park is a popular spot for swimming, snorkeling and kayaking. Man-made Lake Rousseau, just northwest of town, is populated with bass, catfish, specs and stump knockers.

The floodplain forests of the Halpata Tastanaki Preserve are open to bikers, horseback riders and hikers. Manatees gather in the nearby Crystal River and do not seem to mind swimming with snorkelers.

Population: 9,500 (city proper)

Age 45 or Better: 60%

Cost of Living: 24% below the national average

Median Home Price: $285,000

Climate: Summer temperatures reach into the 90s, and winter temperatures are in the 50s, 60s and 70s. The area, on average, receives 53 inches of rain per year.

At Least One Hospital Accepts Medicare Patients? No, but Seven Rivers Regional Medical Center is 11 miles away in Crystal River and accepts Medicare patients.

At Least One Hospital Accredited by Joint Commission? No, but Seven Rivers Regional Medical Center is 11 miles away in Crystal River and is accredited.

Public Transit: No

Crime Rate: Below the national average

Public Library: Yes

Political Leanings: Very conservative

Drawbacks: The tornado risk is 70% higher than the national average.

Notes: Crystal River Mall, a large shopping venue anchor stores, specialty shops and chain restaurants, is 12 miles away. Further shopping and services are in Inverness, 15 miles away.

Coconut Creek

Growing Coconut Creek is an inland city about 15 miles northwest of Fort Lauderdale in southwestern Florida. It is award winning for its environmentalism and eco-conscious outlook and is home to the world's largest butterfly aviary.

Taking its name from the coconut trees that were planted by early

planners, the city boasts an abundance of parks, gardens and canals. Lushly landscaped avenues are common.

Home styles include Mediterranean, Florida cracker and ranch rambler with pastel colored, stucco exteriors. Condominiums are in good supply, and there are some nice, gated communities, including Winston Park.

The downtown is home to The Promenade at Coconut Creek, an open air "lifestyle center" with offices, restaurants and shops. The Seminole Casino, with more than 2,300 Las Vegas style slot machines, is also downtown.

Residents enjoy an active parks and recreation department and a good selection of restaurants. Well regarded Broward College, a community college with some four-year programs, has a beautiful campus here.

Population: 60,000 (city proper)

Age 45 or Better: 45%

Cost of Living: 19% below the national average

Median Home Price: $310,000

Climate: Summer temperatures are in the 80s and 90s with
frequent rainstorms. Winter temperatures are in the 60s and 70s.
On average, the area receives 60 inches of rain per year.

At Least One Hospital Accepts Medicare Patients? No, but several
hospitals that accept Medicare patients are within five miles.

At Least One Accredited by Joint Commission?   No, but several
hospitals that are accredited are within five miles.

Public Transit: Yes

Crime Rate: Below the national average

Public Library: Yes

Political Leanings: Liberal

Drawbacks: Monarch Hill Renewable Energy Park, locally known
as Mt. Trashmore, is a 225-foot-high landfill site located between
Coconut Creek and Deerfield Beach. It occasionally emits odors.

Notes: None

DeBary

Twenty-six miles northeast of Orlando in northeastern Florida,
DeBary is a pleasant community bordered by Lake Monroe, the St.
John's River and the Lower Wekiva River Preserve State Park. The
town is named after Frederick DeBary, a prosperous wine merchant
who settled here in 1871.

Leafy and lush, DeBary is sprinkled with thousands of live oak trees,
cypress trees and magnolia trees. The extensive parks system,

which is anchored by 110-acre River City Nature Park, is a particular point of pride. DeBary is also an official bird sanctuary.

There are modest neighborhoods with older, concrete block ranch ramblers, as well as newer, master-planned developments with beautiful Mediterranean style homes and recently planted palm trees.

Yearly festivals include the Harvest Fall Festival and the Father and Daughter Dance. The Gateway Center for the Arts has a farmers' market, dance performances, theater productions and art workshops.

Restaurant menus include Greek, Italian and seafood cuisines. Shopping is limited and generally takes place in neighboring Sanford or Orange City.

Canaveral National Seashore is just 30 miles away.

Population: 23,000 (city proper)

Age 45 or Better: 50%

Cost of Living: 3% below the national average

Median Home Price: $398,000

Climate: Summers and early fall are hot and humid, while late fall and winter are less humid and cooler. On average, the area receives 55 inches of rain per year.

At Least One Hospital Accepts Medicare Patients? No, but Florida Hospital Fish Memorial in Orange City is five miles away and accepts Medicare patients.

At Least One Hospital is Accredited by Joint Commission? No, but Florida Hospital Fish Memorial in Orange City is five miles away and is accredited.

Public Transit: Yes, provided by Votran, but it is limited. SunRail, a commuter rail system, has a train station in town and travels to Orlando.

Crime Rate: Below the national average

Public Library: Yes

Political Leanings: Liberal

Drawbacks: Parts of DeBary are prone to flooding during hurricanes and tropical storms.

Notes: Lake Monroe is primarily a fishing lake. DeBary has a reputation as a well-managed place.

Deerfield Beach

Deerfield Beach is situated along the congested southeastern Florida coast and started out as an agricultural community. It was named Deerfield for the deer grazing in the fields and remained a farming hub until the 1940s when it changed its name to Deerfield Beach to attract tourists.

Today, the town does attract sun worshippers but not in the numbers seen by some of its neighbors. Clean and often uncrowded, the one-mile-long beach is award-winning and has a 920-foot-long fishing pier. The boardwalk boasts small shops and restaurants with hotels and condominiums across the street.

The city has 19 parks, including Quiet Waters Park, which has water skiing, fishing, mountain bike trails and camping spots. Deerfield Park is a large nature preserve, and the Deerfield Arboretum receives rave reviews.

Downtown is busy with a mix of tall glass office buildings, chain restaurants, banks, parking garages and the like.   The Country

Music Festival and the National Night Out are just two of many community events.

Restaurants are in good supply and include everything from BBQ joints to Italian bistros. Shopping malls include Hillsboro Square, which has nearly 50 retailers.

Housing stock includes modest ranch ramblers, sleek Mediterranean style homes, condominiums and more.

Population: 88,000 (city proper)

Age 45 or Better: 50%

Cost of Living: 23% below the national average

Median Home Price: $290,000

Climate: This area has a tropical monsoon climate. The area receives 58 inches of rain per year, on average.

At Least One Hospital Accepts Medicare Patients? No, but Boca Raton Regional Hospital and North Broward Medical Center are within five miles and accept Medicare patients.

At Least One Hospital is Accredited by Joint Commission? No, but Boca Raton Regional Hospital and North Broward Medical Center are within five miles and are accredited.

Public Transit: Yes, provided by Broward County Transit. A para-transit service is also available.

Crime Rate: Meets the national average

Public Library: Yes

Political Leanings: Liberal

Drawbacks: Hurricanes are always a possibility.

Notes: U.S. Route 1 runs through the city.

Floral City

Platted in 1883, old fashioned Floral City was once the center of Florida's phosphate mining industry.   It is a quiet, country community, about 70 miles north of Tampa in the northwestern part of the state, and it has a nice reputation.

Giant old oak trees shade the main street, and elegant lime rock houses survive in the historic district.   The town center and library are special points of pride.   Businesses include antique stores, motorcycle shops, bike shops, a garden center, a fresh produce stand and a farmers' market.

The Florida Artists Gallery has classes, lectures and a cafe.   Floral City is at the mid-point of the Withlacoochee State Trail and celebrates trail riders with an annual Bikes and BBQ Cook Off.

The town rests on the edge of the Tsala Apopka Lake, a large stretch of lakes, marshes, cypress trees and wildlife habitats.   Two private resorts provide fishing docks and access to the Lake.   Bradley Lake has a boat launch.

Neighborhoods are rural.   Manufactured homes and modest ranch ramblers make up most of the housing stock.

Basic supplies can be found in town, but residents often travel to Inverness, eight miles away, for further shopping and services.

Population: 5,500 (city proper)

Age 45 or Better: 55%

Cost of Living: 23% below national average

Median Home Price: $290,000

Climate: This area has a humid subtropical climate. Summer temperatures are in the 80s and 90s, and winter temperatures are in the 60s and 70s.

At Least One Hospital Accepts Medicare Patients? No, but Citrus Memorial, eight miles away in Inverness, accepts Medicare patients.

At Least One Hospital Accredited by Joint Commission? No, but Citrus Memorial, eight miles away in Inverness, is accredited.

Public Transit: The County has a reservation-based van service.

Crime Rate: Below the national average

Public Library Yes

Political Leanings: Conservative

Drawbacks: The tornado risk is 105% greater than the national average.

Notes: None

Jensen Beach

Situated along the Indian River, just south and east of Port St. Lucie on Florida's southeastern coast, quaint, unassuming Jensen Beach was the "Pineapple Capital of the World" in the late 19th century. These days it is known for its peaceful lifestyle, sea turtles, river fishing and deep-sea fishing.

Neighborhoods are peppered with palm trees and flowering plants. Older, brick residences and pastel-colored homes mingle with new, gated developments. The Falls of Jensen Beach is one such development.

The downtown area along tree lined Jensen Beach Boulevard is busy with traffic but has shops, boat storage facilities and beach bars. Eateries serve jambalaya, shrimp creole, fried oysters and the like.

The city has a sizeable "snowbird" population, and water activities are a way of life. Hutchinson Island, just across the river via a causeway, is home to Jensen Sea Turtle Beach, a wide, oceanfront stretch of sand with amenities and lifeguards. Sections of the beach are roped off to keep humans away from three species of nesting sea turtles.

Residents enjoy two golf courses, a large indoor shopping mall, a Publix grocery, a farmers' market, movie theaters and more. The annual downtown Arts and Crafts Show and the Pineapple Festival draw large crowds.

Population: 14,000 (city proper)

Age 45 or Better: 54%

Cost of Living: Meets the national average

Median Home Price: $420,000

Climate: Summer temperatures are in the 80s and 90s with high humidity levels and frequent rainstorms. Winter temperatures are in the 60s and 70s.

At Least One Hospital Accepts Medicare Patients? No, but Martin Memorial Medical Center, five miles away in Stuart, accepts Medicare patients.

At Least One Accredited by Joint Commission? No, but Martin Memorial Medical Center, five miles away in Stuart, is accredited.

Public Transit: No

Crime Rate: Below the national average

Public Library: Yes

Political Leanings: Conservative

Drawbacks: Hurricanes are always a possibility

Notes: None

Laguna Beach

Low key Laguna Beach is an elongated, unincorporated community on the Florida Panhandle coast, about two miles west of Panama City Beach. On one side of town is the Gulf of Mexico and on the other side is beautiful Conservation Park, a 3,000-acre wetland area with walking trails and a few alligators.

Essentially the quieter side of Panama City Beach, Laguna Beach has a long, wide stretch of sugar white sand tucked against emerald waters. The town is largely residential, and its beach is lined by large homes, vacation rental properties, motels and condominiums.

Neighborhoods are modest with an unfinished feeling. Stubby palm trees line narrow streets without sidewalks, and housing stick includes single story bungalows and conch styles.

Beach access points dot Front Beach Road, which is the main road that runs along the western edge of town. Busy Panama City Beach Parkway travels along the eastern edge. Nearly all services, shopping venues and amenities are in Panama City Beach.

Population: 4,300 (city proper)

Age 45 or Better: 52%

Cost of Living: Meets the national average

Median Home Price: $420,000

Climate: This area has a humid subtropical climate. Summer temperatures are in the 80s and 90s, and winter temperatures are in the 50s, 60s and 70s. On average, the area receives 65 inches of rain per year.

At Least One Hospital Accepts Medicare Patients? No, but Gulf Coast Medical Center, 15 miles away in Panama City, accepts Medicare patients.

At Least One Hospital Accredited by Joint Commission? No, but Gulf Coast Medical Center, 15 miles away in Panama City, is accredited.

Public Transit: A bus runs along Front Beach Road and connects to Panama City Beach.

Crime Rate: Below the national average

Public Library: No

Political Leanings: Very conservative

Drawbacks: Hurricanes are always a possibility.

Notes: Notes

Mary Esther

About 35 miles east of Pensacola, this western Panhandle coastal town is wedged between Fort Walton Beach, Santa Rosa Sound and the U. S. Air Force's Hurlburt Field. It is a generally quiet, suburban place, home to many military personnel and their families.

Mary Esther neighborhoods are neatly laid out and generally tidy with brick ranch ramblers. There are more elaborate waterfront single family homes and condominiums, too, but most residences are inland.

The town manages its own community garden, a welcoming piece of ground that employs sustainable practices such as composting and rainwater collection. Mary Esther also maintains ten public parks, the largest of which is Oak Tree Nature Park. Pier Park includes a boat ramp and fishing facilities.

Santa Rosa Mall is where many residents shop. It is not a fancy place but has enough small stores and national retailers to meet basic needs.

Santa Rosa Island, across the Sound from Mary Esther, is part of the Gulf Islands National Seashore and is open for swimming, bicycling, snorkeling and beach combing. Its Pirate Cove is an excellent place to catch red fish and spotted sea trout.

Population: 4,000 (city proper)

Age 45 or Better: 39%

Cost of Living: 16% below the national average

Median Home Price: $345,000

Climate: Summer temperatures are in the 80s and 90s, and winter temperatures are in the 60s and 70s. On average, Mary Esther receives 65 inches of rain per year.

At Least One Hospital Accepts Medicare Patients? No, but Fort Walton Beach Medical Center, three miles away, accepts Medicare patients.

At Least One Hospital Accredited by Joint Commission? No, but Fort Walton Beach Medical Center, three miles away, is accredited.

Public Transit: Yes

Crime Rate: Below the national average

Public Library: The Mary Esther Public Library has book discussion groups and movie matinees.

Political Leanings: Very conservative

Drawbacks: Hurricanes and tropical storms are always a possibility.

Notes: Mary Esther sits along U.S. Route 98, a primary east-west highway, and the roadway can become very congested during summer tourist season.   This is bear country, and the city works with residents to help them coexist with the growing bear population.

North Port

Originally established by the land development business General Development Company in the late-1950s, North Port straddles the Myakka River in southwestern Florida. It is about an hour north of Fort Myers and an hour and a half south of Tampa. Some of North Port's recent growth has come through annexation of neighboring towns.

The city is suburban and leafy, nearly covered with meandering streets and planned residential neighborhoods that have a mix of young families and retirees. Homes are primarily ranch ramblers.

The part of town not covered by homes is to the southwest and across the river. Here the land gives way to the Myakka State Forest. Dense and lush, the forest is open for bicycling, bird watching, horseback riding, camping, fishing and hiking.

The city has an active parks and recreation department. One of its most popular events is Newcomer Welcome Days for people who have just relocated here or who are considering making the move.

The City Hall is attractive, but there is no real downtown. Merchants include grocery stores, bicycle repair shops, donut shops, a Saturday farmers' market and the like, but most services and shopping venues are in neighboring Charlotte.

Cultural opportunities are in good supply, though. The North Port Chorale has been entertaining residents since 1980, and the North Port Symphony has reasonably priced season concert packages. The North Port Concert Band has a robust schedule and is composed of dedicated volunteers. The North Port Art Center has classes for all ages.

Population: 82,000 (city proper)

Age 45 or Better: 45%

Cost of Living: 4% below the national average

Median Home Price: $395,000

Climate: This area has a humid subtropical climate, meaning two seasons a year. Summer and early fall are hot and humid. Late fall and winter are less humid and cooler.

At Least One Hospital Accepts Medicare Patients? No, but Fawcett Memorial Hospital, nine miles away in Port Charlotte, accepts Medicare patients.

At Least One Hospital Accredited by Joint Commission? No, but Fawcett Memorial Hospital, nine miles away in Charlotte, is accredited.

Public Transit: Yes

Crime Rate: Below the national average

Public Library: Yes

Political Leanings: Conservative

Is Florida Considered Tax Friendly for Retirement? Yes

Drawbacks: The tornado risk is 74% higher than the national average.

Notes: Warm Mineral Springs, located in North Port, is a sink hole that over the years has drawn people hoping to be healed by its mineral-rich waters.

Ormond Beach

Between the Atlantic Ocean and the Halifax River on Florida's northeastern coast, just north of lively Daytona Beach, Ormond

Beach was the winter home of John D. Rockefeller. The industrialist and philanthropist had declared that he would live to be 100 years old and needed a healthy place to live. This was the place that he chose.

Remnants of Ormond Beach's Rockefeller days still stand. In particular, the Casements, Rockefeller's home, is now owned by the city and is a cultural center. The historic downtown is busy and has beautiful gardens, white-washed buildings and a river walk.

Most neighborhoods are tidy, and there are some nice, gated communities. Home styles range from Florida cracker and concrete block ranch rambler to French provincial and Spanish Colonial.

The town is also known as the "Birthplace of Speed" because some of the nation's first automobile races took place on the compacted beach sand. Today the orange-tinted sand is lined by tall hotels and condominiums with beachfront pools. Vehicles are still allowed on certain sections of the beach.

National retailers include Talbot's, Walmart, Publix and more. Specialty shops are plentiful, too. A farmers' market happens every Thursday.

Tomoka State Park is just three miles to the north. It is home to manatees, alligators and 160 bird species.

Population: 45,000 (city proper)

Age 45 or Better: 53%

Cost of Living: Meets the national average

Median Home Price: $419,000

Climate: Summer temperatures are in the 80s and 90s, and winter temperatures are in the 50s, 60s and 70s. On average, the area receives 50 inches of rain per year.

At Least One Hospital Accepts Medicare Patients? Yes

At Least One Hospital Accredited by Joint Commission? No, but Daytona Beach, five miles away, has an accredited hospital.

Public Transit: Yes, provided by Voltran

Crime Rate: Meets the national average

Public Library: Yes

Political Leanings: Liberal

Drawbacks: Hurricanes and tropical storms can happen.

Notes: Although generally a clean and quiet place, Ormond Beach does receive overflow from some of Daytona's rowdy activities, including Bike Week, Spring Break and Speedweeks.

Palm Bay

Low key Palm Bay grew quickly during the 2004 to 2008 housing boom and continues to blossom. It is now the largest metropolis on Florida's Space Coast and is within 30 minutes of Port Canaveral, Florida's second busiest cruise port.

Originally settled at the mouth of Turkey Creek, Palm Bay is named after the sabal palms that grow here, and it is primarily a residential place. Although the city lacks a classic downtown, shopping centers and light industrial parks are scattered here and there.

A large community college campus, a community theater and 2 libraries are also here. Locally owned eateries and national restaurant chains serve everything from seafood to South American cuisine.

Turkey Creek wanders through town, and the Turkey Creek Sanctuary has a boardwalk, a nature center, canoe access points and a mountain bike trail. Wildlife in the Turkey Creek Sanctuary includes ospreys and manatees. Palm Bay's parks and recreation department sponsors an outdoor movie series and food truck wars.

The northeast and northwest areas of the city have older homes in established neighborhood. Newer residences, nicer neighborhoods, better roads and a somewhat rural quality are found in the city's southeast and southwest sections.

Population: 124,000 (city proper)

Age 45 or Better: 35%

Cost of Living: 15% below the national average

Median Home Price: $335,000

Climate: This area has hot, humid summers and mild winters. Summer temperatures are in the 80s and 90s, and winter temperatures are in the 60s and 70s. On average, the area receives 50 inches of rain per year.

At Least One Hospital Accepts Medicare Patients? Yes

At Least One Hospital Accredited by Joint Commission? No, but Holmes Regional Medical Center, about seven miles away in Melbourne, is accredited.

Public Transit: Yes

Crime Rate: Meets the national average

Public Library: Yes

Political Leanings: Conservative

Drawbacks: Certain parts of town are less desirable than others. Much of the narrow beach is privately owned.

Notes: A housing dollar goes a long way here.

Palm Coast

Pleasant Palm Coast sits to the west of the Intracoastal Waterway on Florida's northeastern coast. It started out in the 1960s as a planned retirement community.

This is still primarily a residential place, but the city is developing a new, mixed use town center with parks, paths, retailers, medical offices and housing. Neighborhoods are neatly laid out, and many homes sit along a canal. Residences are mostly cookie cutter concrete block style or Mediterranean style.

The barrier island east of the Intracoastal Waterway is home to the high-end Hammock Beach Resort, which has single family homes and condominiums for sale. Although much of the beach is privately owned by the Resort, residents enjoy a public nature preserve and several beachfront parks with boardwalks and limited water access.

Birdwatching and whale spotting are popular activities, but swimming is not encouraged thanks to hidden coquina rocks and strong undercurrents. Many residents visit Flagler Beach, just 10 miles away, for water activities.

Palm Coast has a farmers' market, a Publix, a Walgreens, a Lowe's the like. A few nicer restaurants are here, but most eateries are casual.

Nightlife is quiet, but the Flagler Playhouse, a community theater, is just 12 miles away in Bunnell.

Population: 95,000 (city proper)

Age 45 or Better: 57%

Cost of Living: 7% below the national average

Median Home Price: $380,000

Climate: This area has hot, humid summers with temperatures in 80s and 90s and mild winters with temperatures in the 50s, 60s and 70s. On average, the area receives 56 inches of rain per year.

At Least One Hospital Accepts Medicare Patients? Yes

At Least One Hospital Accredited by Joint Commission?   Yes

Public Transit: No, but the County provides an on demand, pre-scheduled van service.

Crime Rate: Meets the national average

Public Library: Yes

Political Leanings: Conservative

Drawbacks: Hurricanes are a possibility, but the risk in this area is less than in more southern coastal towns. The tornado risk is 40% higher than the national average.

Notes: Palm Coast has a lot of "snowbirds."

Port Salerno

Settled in the 1920s by Italian immigrants, amiable, suburban Port Salerno sits on the St. Lucie River Inlet in southeastern Florida and straddles the Manatee Pocket, a quiet, scenic bay.   Its proximity to the Atlantic Ocean has made Port Salerno an excellent base for commercial fishing, a tradition that continues today.

Port Salerno is a perfect base for recreational fisherman, too, as sea bass, grouper, kingfish, mutton snapper are particularly plentiful. The town is known for its wonderful seafood festival, which features great food, live entertainment and arts and crafts.

The Manatee Pocket waterfront boasts a cluster of ship builders, marinas, fishing charter companies and seafood restaurants. It is also home to the Fish House Art Center, a company in which artists operate galleries and studios.

The nearby St. Lucie Inlet Preserve Park, which is directly east of town, has white sand beaches that are important sea turtle nesting areas.   The Anastasia Rock Reef extends along the Park's waters and is ideal for snorkeling or SCUBA diving. A boardwalk wanders from the Park's dock to the beach.

The Chapman School of Seamanship offers classes to professional and amateur mariners alike.

Home styles are mostly frame ranch rambler, concrete block ranch rambler and Florida cracker.

Population: 12,500 (city proper)

Age 45 or Better: 50%

Cost of Living: 1% below the national average

Median Home Price: $415,000

Climate: This area has a humid subtropical climate. Summer temperatures are in the 80s and 90s, and winter temperatures are in the 60s and 70s. On average, the area receives 58 inches of rain per year.

At Least One Hospital Accepts Medicare Patients? No, but Stuart, about three miles away, has a hospital that accepts Medicare patients.

At Least One Accredited by Joint Commission? No, but Jupiter, about 15 miles away, has a hospital that is accredited.

Public Transit: Yes, but it is limited.

Crime Rate: Below the national average

Public Library: No, but Stuart, about three miles away, has a public library.

Political Leanings: Conservative

Drawbacks: Hurricanes and tropical storms are always a possibility.

Notes: Port Salerno is popular with "snowbirds." Most shopping and services are in nearby Stuart.

San Antonio

San Antonio is a safe, fast-growing town just to the west of Lake Jovita in west central Florida. About 30 miles north of Tampa, it was founded as a Catholic colony in 1881 and is the only surviving community out of five original villages.

Agriculture, particularly orange groves, has long sustained San Antonio, and the town still has a rural, slightly overgrown quality with leafy neighborhoods and lush pastureland just beyond its boundaries. Housing stock is a mix of older concrete block style homes and new, polished country club residences.

San Antonio Liquors, also known as Ralph's, has a restaurant and live music Friday and Saturday nights, and GarageMahal is where the sounds of acoustic guitars, fiddles, banjos and mandolins come together on weekends.

Events include the Art and Wine Fest, a casual but fun affair. The Rattlesnake Festival brings out nearly everyone for food, arts and crafts and snake shows.

The dining scene is primarily made up of BBQ smokehouses and pizza places. Retailers include a pottery shop, a lumber store, shoe stores, clothiers, bicycle shops and a few others.

Population: 1,500 (city proper)

Age 45 or Better: 35%

Cost of Living: 4% below the national average

Median Home Price: $398,000

Climate: Summer and early fall are hot and humid. Late fall and winter are less humid and cooler. On average, the area receives 55 inches of rain per year.

At Least One Hospital Accepts Medicare Patients? No, but Pasco Regional Medical Center, five miles away, accepts Medicare patients.

At Least One Hospital Accredited by Joint Commission?   No, but Pasco Regional Medical Center, five miles away, is accredited.

Public Transit: No

Crime Rate: Below the national average

Public Library: No

Political Leanings: Conservative

Drawbacks: The tornado risk is 135% higher than the national average.

Notes: San Antonio is essentially a Tampa exurb. St. Leo University, a private, Catholic liberal arts university with 17,000 students, is in St. Leo just to the east of San Antonio.

Sebastian

Sleepy Sebastian sits along the Indian River Lagoon on southwestern Florida's Treasure Coast.   A quiet, simple place, Sebastian is the site of America's first wildlife refuge, Pelican Island.

The waterfront is clean, grassy and has a modern fishing pier. Surfing, boating and saltwater fishing for redfish, bluefish and Spanish mackerel are favorite pastimes.

Restaurants range from cozy, family run eateries, including the wonderful Red Rooster Café, to funky biker dives.   Retailers include Winn Dixie, Publix, Home Depot and Walgreens.   Many residents drive to Vero Beach, 13 miles away, for services and shopping at the Indian River Mall.

Thick, wild and wet, St. Sebastian River Preserve borders the city to the west.   It is the place for horseback riding, canoeing, hiking and camping.   Sebastian Inlet State Park to the east is a favorite with fishermen, and Pelican Island National Wildlife Refuge to the southeast is home to swamps, mangroves and hundreds of bird species.

Neighborhoods have a mix of modest ranch ramblers, newer gated communities and riverfront developments.

Six nearby beaches, three with facilities and three without, are often nearly empty on weekdays.

Population: 27,000 (city proper)

Age 45 or Better: 50%

Cost of Living: 8% below the national average

Median Home Price: $375,000

Climate: Summer temperatures are in the 80s and 90s, and winter temperatures are in the 60s and 70s. On average, the area receives 55 inches of rain per year.

At Least One Hospital Accepts Medicare Patients? Yes

At Least One Hospital Accredited by Joint Commission? Yes

Public Transit: Yes

Crime Rate: Below the national average

Public Library: Yes

Political Leanings: Conservative

Drawbacks: The area is vulnerable to hurricanes and tropical storms.

Notes: None

Stuart

Friendly, mellow Stuart sits on southeastern Florida's Treasure Coast. Once a pirates' lair, today it has a thriving boating and charter fishing industry and is known as the "Sailfish Capital of the World."

Tourists come not just to fish but also to dive and sail. New residents have come, too, increasing Stuart's population by 4% in the last decade.

Yet, unlike some of its neighbors to the south, Stuart has not yet been overbuilt. It has a nice river walk, and its cute downtown has awning draped shops, galleries, eateries and a farmers' market. The shopping mall has national retailers.

The Elliott Museum, the Barn Theatre and the Lyric Theatre provide a touch of culture. The Stuart Boat Show happens every January and showcases 500 boats of every shape and size.

Housing includes everything from waterfront mansions to modest condominiums and concrete block ranch ramblers.

With its wide strip of sand, very blue water and up to date facilities, Stuart Beach is one of the best in the County.

Population: 18,000 (city proper)

Age 45 or Better: 54%

Cost of Living: Meets the national average

Median Home Price: $420,000

Climate: Stuart sits in a transition zone between tropical and subtropical climates. On average, the area receives 57 inches of rain each year.

At Least One Hospital Accepts Medicare Patients? Yes

At Least One Hospital Accredited by Joint Commission? Yes

Public Transit: Yes, provided by Martin County

Crime Rate: Meets the national average

Public Library: Yes

Political Leanings: Conservative

Drawbacks: At least three hurricanes have brushed Stuart since 2004.

Notes: People seem to enjoy living in Stuart.

Tavares

Located in north central Florida, about 30 miles northwest of Orlando, semi-rural Tavares bills itself as "America's Seaplane City." It borders four large lakes and has several smaller ones within town limits.

Water events and activities abound and include cypress swamp eco-cruises, a bass tournament, a race boat regatta, an antique boat show, a dragon boat show, Jet Ski races and many others. Seaplane fly-ins attract pilots from around the region and feature contests for "shortest take off," "best spot landing" and more.

The forty-slip Seaplane Base and Marina is in the simple but renovated downtown and is owned by the city. Wooten Park, along Lake Dora, has a boat dock, a popular water park and huge live oaks with dripping moss. Wooten is also the site of the Tuesday morning farmers' market.

Residents enjoy a sushi restaurant, a pizzeria, a Cajun place and a bar or two. Shopping venues are limited.

Most neighborhoods are modest with older, concrete block ranch ramblers, but there are also new subdivisions with modern home designs. Many residences, new and old, are located on a lake or in a lakeside community with water access.

Population: 20,000 (city proper)

Age 45 or Better: 60%

Cost of Living: 17% below the national average

Median Home Price: $345,000

Climate: Tavares has a humid subtropical climate with 48 inches of rainfall each year. Summers temperatures are in the 80s and 90s, and winters are mild with temperatures in the 50s, 60s and 70s.

At Least One Hospital Accepts Medicare Patients? Yes

At Least One Hospital Accredited by Joint Commission?   Yes

Public Transit: Yes

Crime Rate: Below the national average

Public Library: Yes

Political Leanings: Conservative

Drawbacks: The tornado risk is 126% higher than the national average.

Notes: Tavares is a nice town for the price.

Yulee

Not too long ago, Yulee, 25 miles northeast of Jacksonville in northeastern Florida, was just a sleepy country hamlet. Today, it is a collection of new subdivisions, but it still retains much of its rural ambiance.

Marshes and inlets border Yulee on its eastern edge, and fifteen minutes beyond these are the beaches of Fernandina Beach and Amelia Island. They are easy to reach and are the reasons many people want to live here.

Yulee's older homes are small but reflect Old Florida, with screened-in porches, raised floors and lush lots. Newer areas have neatly laid out streets, fewer trees, ranch ramblers and single story and two-story Mediterranean style homes, many with marsh views. Between neighborhoods, wooded land remains home to nature's wild creatures.

Fast food places, diners and national retailers, including Target, Winn-Dixie, Kohl's, Home Depot and more, are found on Route AIA (the Buccaneer Trail) that runs through the center of town. A few locally owned restaurants are here and there.

Yulee has a nine-hole golf course. Another seven courses are within a short drive.

Population: 14,000 (city proper)

Age 45 or Better: 34%

Cost of Living: 2% below the national average

Median Home Price: $410,000

Climate: Summer temperatures are in the 80s and 90s. Winter temperatures are in the 50s, 60s and 70s. On average, the area receives 51 inches of rain per year.

At Least One Hospital Accepts Medicare Patients? No, but Fernandina Beach has a hospital that accepts Medicare patients.

At Least One Hospital Accredited by Joint Commission?   No, but Fernandina Beach has an accredited hospital.

Public Transit: Nassau County's Council on Aging has a van transportation system with service to medical appointments and more.

Crime Rate: Below the national average

Public Library: Yes

Political Leanings: Very, very conservative

Drawbacks: None

Notes: Yulee is home to the Nassau County Courthouse and to Florida State College's Betty Cook Nassau Center, which has a Center for Lifelong Learning. Interstate 95 is just west of town and provides direct access into Jacksonville.

Thanks for reading!

About the Author

Kris Kelley lives in beautiful Colorado has been finding and reviewing great places to retire since 2006. She is an avid traveler, always looking for that hidden gem of a town, whether it be along an ocean, in a desert or on a mountaintop!

More Titles by the Author

45 Affordable Retirement Towns: Best U.S. Towns for Retirement on a Budget

35 Affordable Waterfront Retirement Towns: Best U.S. Towns for an Affordable Retirement along a Lake, River or Seacoast

18 Affordable Southwestern Retirement Towns: Best Southwestern Towns for Retirement on a Budget

Made in United States
North Haven, CT
19 August 2023

40491645R00039